# 10 Powerful Stress Busters

## For the **BAM VP** Woman in You

BARBARA MITCHELL, DCH

*10 Powerful Stress Busters* by Barbara Mitchell, DCH

http://www.thecalmingbreath.com

Copyright © 2013 by Barbara Mitchell, DCH

All Rights Reserved

Dr Barbara DCH LLC

ISBN: 978-0-9820209-5-1 Paperback Edition

# What Others Are Saying

"I wish more people would understand the rest and relaxation is pivotal to good health. We seem to be rushing around more and with so many technological gadgets controlling our lives and raising our stress levels. There are people who can't do without a phone, etc. I hope individuals who read your book, could step back and realize the message; it's about healing the mind,body,and soul."
**Lorna Ryan**

Dear Dr. Barbara,
"I can't tell you and thank you enough for writing "10 Powerful Stress Busters for the BAM VP Woman in You". Just reading the whole book, I found myself releasing my stress through meditation and communing with God as I walked on my treadmill. I can honestly say that the many techniques you offered really gives you hope and lets you know that you are not alone. Interestingly enough, your book re-introduces yourself to yourself because somewhere in time you have forgotten who you really were. I loved the quotations you used for each topic. Especially the quotation from Eddie Cantor, "Slow down and enjoy life. It's not only the scenery you miss by going too fast-you also miss the sense of where you are going and why." Moreover the suggested techniques at the conclusion of each topic was a bonus. Thank you for an excellent and helpful book whom I would gladly recommend to everyone."
**~Tiffany McCullough**

"This is an excellent book that teaches you in very simple terms how to use easy remedies  to slow your busy life down. She backs up her work with different links to further help you along your journey to calm your life and your world down a bit. She talks about how stress is a major cause of many disease states and how to relax the mind and body through different modalities. For instance, breath is the easiest thing to control in a tight situation, the author, Dr Barbara, tells you step by step how to breathe effectively in order to calm down. One of the things I did right after I read her book, was putting some lemon essential oil in a pot of water, let it simmer, and enjoyed the citrus aroma throughout my home. Citrus is not only a clean scent, but it's uplifting as well. She talks about Reiki, Self-hypnotherapy. There are quite a few modalities to choose from, certain to relax, rejuvenate, and calm the spirit. A well written book! I look forward to reading the next one."
**~Kim Ford**

"For anyone who is new to stress management and who is committed to improving their health and the quality of their life, this book will save them from having to do years of research. Just like I always carry my purse for survival whenever I leave the house, now I also always carry the book's recommended techniques of BAM VP a handy acronym that reminds me where to start de-stressing and how to move through the process. So whether I'm stuck in traffic or negotiating with a used car

salesman I know how to Breathe (deeply), Affirm (my goodness and that of others), Meditate, Visualize (my nervous system responds immediately to pictures of success), Progressively release excess tension from head to toe. Then I feel that I become the book's alternate version of the acronym which is Become A More Vibrant Person because, as the book says, stress can work for me making my life sweeter. I can see how this book would work for teenagers in preparing them to handle a lifetime of stressful situations. And men will also benefit from understanding the way stress works and how to control or to manage it."
**~Maryetta Johnson**

# CONTENTS

Acknowledgments ................................................. i

Introduction ...................................................... ii

Chapter :1    From PMS to Post Menopause:
What Every Woman Should Know About Stress ............... 13

Chapter 2:    Relax – Renew – Refresh – Reenergize.................... 17

Chapter 3:    Cool Calm And Relaxed .................................... 21

Chapter 4:    Spell Stressed Backwards And You Get Desserts: How To
Manage Stress To Make Life Sweeter ......................... 25

Chapter 5:    Empowering Self-Talk: How To Make Affirmations That
Inspire Change ............................................... 29

Chapter 6:    Hypnosis: A Powerful Relaxation Therapy ................... 33

Chapter 7:    EFT: What Is It And Why Should You Care? ............... 35

Chapter 8:    Aromatherapy: A Natural Way To Boost Your Mood ........ 39

Chapter 9:    A 5 Minute Morning Meditation To Lift Your Spirits And
Put A Smile On Your Face ................................... 41

Chapter 10:    Bonus: Be A More Vibrant Person: How To Fit Relaxation
Into Your Busy Day............................................ 45

Recapture Your Joy of Living ................................. 49

About the Author............................................. 51

"Give your stress wings and let it fly away"

~Terry Guillemets

# ACKNOWLEDGMENTS

Fred, my super spouse, thank you for always supporting my creative works.  And most of all for knowing how and when to offer constructive suggestions :-).
All my love.

# INTRODUCTION

**"It's so important to know that you can choose to feel good. Most people don't think they have that choice". ~Neil Simon**

Welcome to *Ten Powerful Stress Busters for the BAM VP Woman in You.* You are invited to try all of these wellness techniques, selected from the best of my Stress Free Moments blog. You will learn natural methods for reducing the stress, anxiety and tension that is so much a part of our 21st century fast paced lifestyle. Topics from aromatherapy to visualization will be highlighted, with special emphasis on simple, effective breath work for an immediate *relaxation response.

Do you remember that jingle, "I can take home the bacon, fry it up in the pan and never let you forget you're a man. Cause I'm a woman?" I was one of those women. Juggling a career, home, parenting and studying for a degree. Major stress. Trying not to burnout. That is why my message is especially for all women trying to balance the multiple roles of wife, mother, working woman, caregiver, and more.

Chronic stress is no joke. It can lead to severe health problems from burnout, illness and disease. While the stress management techniques in this book have proven effective in reducing stress, they are not a substitute for the advice of your health professional. Always seek medical advice with any stress-related illness. That being said, many hospitals and physicians advise learning stress management to reduce the side effects of medical and surgical procedures.

The good news is that the *Ten Powerful Stress Busters for the BAM VP Woman in You* are fast, effective and uncomplicated stress relief tips and techniques. They are easy to learn. Most take five minutes or less, require no special equipment and can easily fit into an already too busy schedule. Tools you can use right away. Give them a try. Then pick the ones that work best for you.

My message and my desire are to make a difference in the way you handle stress from this day forward. It is wellness made simple with some easy preventative techniques for long-term results. I use them. And have seen amazing results helping family, friends and clients experiencing emotional distress, anxiety, grief and overwhelm go from despair to once again recapture the joy of living.

The *Ten Powerful Stress Busters for the BAM VP Woman in You* are the tools I use to bring back the bold, awesome, motivated, vibrant and passion in you!   Want less stress and more BAM VP in your life? The choice is yours.

For the next few moments, the outside world does not concern you. This is your time. Your space. Your place for relaxation. Find your quiet space.

---

*For more in-depth information on simple, effective mind/body approaches to relieve stress read *The Relaxation Response* by Dr. Herbert Benson

# CHAPTER 1

## FROM PMS TO POST MENOPAUSE: WHAT EVERY WOMAN SHOULD KNOW ABOUT STRESS

**"I am strong, I am invincible, I am woman"**
**song lyric by Helen Reddy**

Last week's horoscope read, "The biggest threat to you is stress – and that's something you can manage if you put your mind to it". Finding ways to manage stress is wise advice for all of us. But when it comes to women's health, practicing some form of stress relief is crucial.

Stress exacerbates a woman's cycle from pre adolescence to post menopause. That is because hormones like estrogen rule our cycles. Add to it the stress hormone cortisol, which is produced in abundance when we become overwhelmed juggling the responsibilities of home, family and career. These hormones make a volatile mix that affects balance, mood changes, changes in metabolism, heart rate, respiration, blood pressure, and memory.

Stress also makes PMS symptoms worse. Extreme levels of stress trigger psychological and physical symptoms during ovulation and menstruation such as cramping, mood swings, fatigue, insomnia, rapid heartbeat and shortness of breath.

Menopause symptoms such as night sweats and hot flashes are far more intense for women under chronic stress.

According to Dr. Susan Lark and other authorities on women's health, the underlying cause of over eighty percent of doctor's visits is stress. Chronic stress can increase one's susceptibility to virtually every major disease.

Studies now link urinary infections, postpartum depression, acnes, psoriasis, diabetes and autoimmune illnesses with chronic stress symptoms. Studies show an indirect link between stress and cancer because chronic stress weakens the immune system – the body's natural defense to contain and destroy cancer cells. Recent research from The Association for Cancer Research links stress to an aggressive form of breast cancer in African American and Latino women.

The problem is that many women don't hear the warning message their bodies send out. Partly because women are too stressed out to listen. They don't connect the symptoms to stress. But the irritability, insomnia, appetite changes, tense muscles they experience are signs of stress.

The good news is there is something you can do today to relieve stress in your life. Try several relaxation techniques to find what works for you. Yoga, meditation, deep breathing, journaling, walks in the park, a hobby, pampering spa treatments, etc. Reassess your to-do list and cross off all the nonessentials. And ask for help when needed.

We now know that taking time to relieve the stress and tension in our lives is not just a "guilty pleasure". Managing stress is vital to our emotional and physical fitness. So start now and dedicate time for relaxation and stress relief, knowing you are contributing to your health and wellness.

Remember, the biggest threat to you is stress. And that's something you can manage if you put your mind to it.

## Suggested Actions You can Take

➤ Make a commitment to yourself to practice some form of relaxation every day.

➤ Find a routine you can stick with that fits your lifestyle.

➤ Practice daily, consistently until managing stress becomes your habit.

➤ Monitor your self- talk when tempted to skip out. Make an affirmation like, "I am doing this everyday … for me and my health" to keep you motivated.

➤ The Holmes-Rahe Stress Scale[1] a free online assessment, measures the impact of stressful life changes you may have experienced over the past year.

[1] The Holmes –Rahe Stress Scale:
http://www.mindtools.com/pages/article/newTCS_82.htm

# CHAPTER 2

## RELAX – RENEW – REFRESH - REENERGIZE

**"Give your stress wings and let it fly away".~Terri Guillemets**

When my daughter was an infant, watching her sleep, her natural breathing pattern sometimes alarmed me. When she inhaled her little stomach would puff up (like blowing air into a balloon) and when she exhaled her stomach deflated, the belly button pulled in tight. Little did I know then, but she knew exactly how to do natural abdominal breathing.

### Take a Deep Breath…and Exhale

Most adults chest breathe. That is we take quick shallow breaths from the upper chest. Take a moment to observe your breathing. Especially when you are nervous or tense. Those shallow breaths cause excess loss of $CO_2$ and deprive your heart and lungs from delivering adequate oxygen to the cells. But when you take slow, deep breaths the fine balance of oxygen and carbon dioxide is restored. When you are under stress this will quickly soothe the nervous system, relax tense muscles and slow a rapidly beating heart.

### Deep Breathing Technique

Breath work is the master key to good health, affecting our

digestion, circulation, blood pressure and energy levels. The technique is easy to master:

Sit in a comfortable position. Loosen any tight clothing. Remove shoes, belts, ties – everything restrictive. Then,

1. Place your hand softly on your stomach.

2. Beginning on the exhalation, notice your stomach pull in as you expel air from your body.

3. Inhale slowly. As air fills your stomach imagine blowing up a balloon.

4. Allow the breath to travel upward to the chest. Then exhale slowly.

5. Take a normal breath.

6. Repeat several times until you get the desired results.

This deep breathing technique has left you feeling relaxed and that's a good thing. Many people who practice it believe we are all born with a predetermined number of life's breaths. And if we are constantly in a state of anxiety or agitation, the consequent rapid breathing is wasting our life force.

## A Calming Breath

So let us continue with this feeling of relaxation through calm breathing. Breathe in relaxation, calmness, coolness, love. Breathe out tension, worry, stress, negativity. This is your time…your space…your place for relaxation.

May this positive energy be with you throughout your day. Namaste.

## Suggested Actions You Can Take

➢ Periodically during the day, ideally every time you change activities, take a minute to relax and recharge. Especially when you are feeling tense and overwhelmed. Put the to-do list on hold. Sit comfortably and focus on your breathing. You will soon notice how much easier it is to handle those frustrating moments.

➢ Enjoy the ultimate relaxation experience. Visit http://thecalmingbreath.com for access to your Bonus Gift: *The Calming Breath 5- Minute Guided Meditation Video*. **Yes it's free!**

# CHAPTER 3

## COOL CALM AND RELAXED

**"Sometimes the most important thing in a whole day is the rest
we take between two deep breaths." ~Etty Hillesum**

You don't need the headlines to tell you these are stressful
times. The mortgage crisis, jobs lost, inadequate health care,
Wall Street and bank bailouts. If you are not directly affected,
you probably know someone who is.

On top of that you've got your own "stuff" – family and other
responsibilities - and the stress begins to take its toll. The outward
signs may be hard to detect at first, but one sure sign of stress can be
seen in your eyes.

Take a look directly at your eyes through a mirror. Normally you
see the whites on either side of the iris. If the whites are visible under
the irises, that could be a symptom of high stress. If you see the
upper whites of your eyes, above the irises, that is a sign of chronic
stress. These signs mean you need to take care of your overall health
– today.

In addition, make time in your schedule to rest and release some
of that stress and anxiety. Learn to relax in any situation using two
simple techniques:

## Rest Your Eyes and Clear Your Mind:

Reiki, or energy therapy (sometimes called healing touch) is an ancient Japanese healing tradition for stress reduction and relaxation. "Reiki Hands" is a quick technique you can do when you need a deeply relaxing break.

> Sit comfortably. Place your elbows on a desk or table. Vigorously rub and clap your hands together to create warmth. Cup your hands over your eyes. Take slow deep breaths and try to see nothing but black.

Tibetan yogis believe that black is the color for optimum relaxation of the optic nerve. Stay with this exercise a few minutes or until you feel relaxed enough to continue with your day.

## Stop Feeling Overwhelmed

NLP or Neuro Linguistic Programming is the study of how language, both verbal and nonverbal affects our nervous system, thoughts and emotions. By using a simple NLP signal, you can change from feeling nervous, tense and overwhelmed to relaxed and centered in minutes.

> First, touch your thumb to forefinger making an "OK" sign. Close your eyes and take a deep breath. As you slowly exhale say to yourself, "I am calm and relaxed. The outside world does not concern me right now. This is my time for serene, calm and relaxed thoughts". Repeat until you begin to feel sensations of relaxation. Mentally go to your place of special memories – a favorite vacation for example. Allow a few moments to feel good about yourself.

## Cool, Calm and Relaxed

The next time you hear news that makes you tense, stressed or angry, notice where you feel it on your body. Stomach in knots? Tightness in the chest?  Pain in the neck and shoulders?  Wherever you feel it, try the following technique for relief:

Close your eyes and mentally get in touch with the area of discomfort. Visualize/imagine that this feeling has a size, shape and color. First, begin to manipulate the **size. Make** it longer, shorter, wider and finally small as a dot. Next, make the shape smoother, rounder, then weightless. Imagine the color lighter, brighter, softer…billowy and airy. Now allow this airy feeling to travel up your body. Imagine it reaching the back of your throat. At that moment take a deep breath, purse your lips and forcefully blow it out of your body! Really blow.

Mentally scan your body. Do you still feel tense, stressed or angry? If so, close your eyes and repeat this technique a few times until the feeling is gone. Now you are in control - cool, calm and relaxed.

## You Deserve to Be Happy and Healthy

Think in terms of your health and well-being. Then take time out…for you. Whether you are in a state of high stress, chronic stress, or just have a desire to be proactive in managing stress, the above relaxation techniques will give you relief during stressful times.

## Suggested Actions You Can Take

If you are like most of us your day begins about 7:00 a.m. and does not end until 10:00 or 11:00 p.m. That's approximately sixteen hours or 960 available minutes a day.

➢ Carve five minutes out of your day to take a relaxation break.

➢ Even better- every time you change activities throughout the day, take a couple of minutes to relax.

➢ You'll feel better and more in control.

23

# CHAPTER 4

## SPELL STRESSED BACKWARDS AND YOU GET DESSERTS:  HOW TO MANAGE STRESS TO MAKE LIFE SWEETER

**"Slow down and enjoy life. It's not only the scenery you miss by going too fast – you also miss the sense of where you are going and why." ~Eddie Cantor, comedian**

Let's face it. We are all going to face some stress in our lives. Although not all stress is bad. A new home, job promotion, new baby, wedding plans are all examples of good stress. On the other hand tight finances and job losses are all too common sources of stress in these economic times. These negative events take a mental and physical toll on us. This can eventually impact our immune system and lead to long-term health problems.

### How Do You Cope with Stress

So how do you cope when faced with stressful situations?  How do you get through the day?  Do things build until you find yourself with a short fuse, easily irritated, taking your anger out on those around you? Or are you one who becomes overwhelmed, emotionally withdrawn, depressed and end up doing nothing?

In either case, you probably know you need better coping skills. A skill that is both powerful and effective is a technique used in NLP called "anchoring" The premise of this procedure is that you can change the way you feel immediately – sad to happy, lethargic to motivated for example – by using anchors. The process is really quite simple. And it works. Here is how to do it.

## Stop Negative Self Talk

The next time you are feeling down change the way you physically carry yourself. Hold your head up, stand tall, breathe deeply and walk with confidence. Sounds too simple, right? But notice the reaction you get when interacting with others. Your outward appearance will project confidence no matter how you feel inside.

Next change your negative self-talk – the "loser" talk – with one word. STOP! See the word mentally or speak it out loud. This will immediately interrupt that downward spiral and pave the way for anchoring.

## NLP Anchoring

Start by remembering a time you felt good about yourself. Proud, strong, confident, loved. Immerse yourself in that memory. What were you doing, wearing, with whom, saying what. At the height of that memory, when you are feeling awesome, do something unique to anchor that mood. Clench your fists, tug your ear, hum a special tune. Pick a gesture that works for you. Anchor several feel-good memories, dreams or fantasies in the exact same way. And you are done.

Now every time you use your anchor – for example let's say tug your ear – you will automatically trigger all the good feelings you have linked to it.

Use this NLP technique every time you are feeling tense, anxious, stressed. Fire off that anchor and immediately be in a better place. You will feel more resourceful in this state of mind. Better able to explore new avenues for resolving or at least tackling the source of your stress. Look at it this way, when you spell stressed backwards you get desserts. Stress, when managed well, makes life sweeter.

## Suggested Action You Can Take

If you want to learn more about neuro-linguistic programming (NLP) you can watch practitioners demonstrate NLP techniques on Youtube.com

# CHAPTER 5

## EMPOWERING SELF-TALK: HOW TO MAKE AFFIRMATIONS THAT INSPIRE CHANGE

### "Change Your Thoughts and Change Your World" ~Norman Vincent Peale

"Every day in every way I am getting better and better". You probably heard this famous affirmation popularized in the 1920's by Emil Coue, a French pharmacist and psychologist. After observing his patients heal faster when they focused their mind on positive healing images, Coue developed this therapeutic method he called optimistic autosuggestion. His belief that, "you are what you think" proved to have great success in rehabilitating the thousands of patients he treated each year.

You might ask what makes this deceptively simple affirmation so powerful. And how can I duplicate it?

Start with the area you want to work on. Emil Coue addressed the health concerns of people who were ill and wanted to get well. Your challenge may be with finances, career, family, relationships, physical or emotional health, etc. Define your source of stress.

> ➤ Make your affirmation simple and specific. Coue's autosuggestion is a simply stated imagery for healing. Yours

may contain specific relaxation instructions, or suggestions for improved self-esteem or a mantra for success. Make sure it describes exactly what you want to achieve. For example you want to ask for a raise, "I am clear and direct asking my boss for a raise".

➤ Powerful affirmations are positive and carefully expressed. Phrase them as if they are occurring now. Notice Coue says, "I am getting better and better." Avoid negative statements. For example instead of "I will not be nervous asking for a raise". Use a positive version such as "I am letting go of tension when I talk to my boss" or "I am calm and assertive asking for a raise."

➤ An affirmation works best when combined with an image or mental picture. So write it down, close your eyes and visualize the touch, taste and feel of the change you want to create.

➤ Repeat your affirmation throughout the day, every day. The more you say it the more connected it becomes to your desired outcome. Routine repetition was an important part of Coue's method. He recommended his patients repeat "Every day in every way I am getting better and better" upon awakening, throughout the day and before going to sleep at night. When he put the power of healing into the hands of his patients Coue had great success curing them of illness and disease.

Affirmations are good for your mental health. Evidence proves that serotonin and endorphins, those feel good hormones, are released when we focus on positive thoughts. This scientifically based evidence works even if you are a skeptic.

So take a cue from Emil Coue. Practice positive thinking. Make affirmations that work to improve your life. You have nothing to lose but time and everything to gain. Like a happier outlook on life, less anxiety, and better health. The power to change is in you.

## Suggested Actions You Can Take

➢   Practice daily affirmations. Positive words about yourself to yourself. "Today I am (bold, awesome, motivated, vibrant, passionate)". You fill in the words. And find your voice.

➢   You will change the way you feel about yourself.

➢   You project a positive attitude,

➢   Your attitude influences the way you talk to people around you.

➢   You positively impact everyone who comes in contact with you by the way you carry yourself.

# CHAPTER 6

## HYPNOSIS: A POWERFUL RELAXATION THERAPY

**"Real beauty is found in oneself. That's the tranquil beach. The beautiful sunset. It's not a location, the location is you…"**
**~Miles Patrick Yohnke**

When I ask clients if they have ever been hypnotized, invariably they will answer no. But in fact people go in and out of hypnosis every day.

Think about it. When you are daydreaming you are focused inward. That's a natural state of hypnosis. When you are engrossed in a good book and the children are yelling and the dog is barking, but you are oblivious to all around you. That's a natural state of hypnosis. How about when you are in a movie theatre full of people. When the lights go down, it's just you and Denzel or Brad Pitt on that screen. You are so narrowly focused that no one around you exists. A natural state of hypnosis.

Narrowly focused inward, aware of but oblivious to outside stimuli – that is the definition of hypnosis. Specifically, it is a state of focused concentration characterized by very pleasant feelings of relaxation, heightened imagination and increased responsiveness to an idea. While you are fully conscious, you are tuned out to most stimuli around you.

As a Stress Management Consultant, I was attracted to the study of hypnosis because it is a powerful relaxation therapy that helps people make rapid changes. A person with a lifelong fear of flying, for example, can take a plane trip after hypnosis. A person battling weight gain will lose her craving for fattening foods. A heavy smoker will throw away his cigarettes. A person suffering chronic pain can learn to manage it through self-hypnosis and live a better quality of life. A person burdened by a past mistake, trauma, abuse or guilt can have those painful memories neutralized through hypnosis and get to enjoy living life again.

Google "hypnosis" and you will find many scientific studies trying to define how hypnosis works. Using neuroimaging tools scientists do know that it is not a sleep state. The brain waves are in alpha (relaxed) rhythm as opposed to delta (sleep) rhythm. A hypnotized subject when told a white sheet of paper is red shows activation in the color perception area of the brain. Hypnotically induced suggestions of pain activate the brain area as if the subject was in real pain. The phenomenon of inducing goose bumps on the arm of a hypnotized subject by pretending to rub an ice cube on the arm has been observed and documented.

While the scientific studies of hypnotic phenomena are ongoing let me share this anecdotal story. While practicing self-hypnosis I had taught her, my client realized a wonderful side benefit. The pain from blinding migraine headaches she had been experiencing all her adult life were relieved through hypnosis. At her next appointment she reported this to me. Her astonished declaration was, "I don't know how …but this hypnosis stuff really works!"

---

## Suggested Action You Can Take

Are you hypnotizable? Most people think they cannot be hypnotized. But studies show an astonishing 95% can be. What about you? Take the fun quiz sponsored by the International Medical and Dental Hypnotherapy Association and know for sure. http://www.imdha.com

# CHAPTER 7

## EFT: WHAT IS IT AND WHY SHOULD YOU CARE?

**"While we may not be able to control all that happens to us, we can control what happens inside us." ~Benjamin Franklin**

Your boss has asked you to make a speech for him at the next board meeting. You graciously accept. But inside you are freaking out. You are terrified of speaking in public. Every time you think about it your heart pounds and you get a sick feeling in the pit of your stomach. The stress is causing you sleepless nights. Is there any way to handle this panicky feeling so you can make the speech?

### Emotional Freedom Technique

Here is where EFT comes in. Founded by Gary Craig in the mid 90's, EFT is an acronym for Emotional Freedom Technique. It is a self-help procedure for quickly releasing emotional distress and traumatic memories by neutralizing the fears and phobias that trigger them. The end product is to defuse the emotional charge so the distress or trauma no longer has power over us.

EFT has been used to alleviate performance anxiety, fear of heights, panic attacks, sports performance, cravings and compulsions, animal phobias and more. Its ability to enhance the outcome on health issues, psychological problems and performance issues has been scientifically studied and presented in peer review journals, research and outcome studies. EFT success stories have been reported on TV, magazine and newspaper articles.

## So Easy You Can Do It

EFT is easy to learn and apply. You use your finger to gently tap on certain points of the body. The impact is similar to acupuncture but without the needles. The best part is you can do it yourself in minutes and get results even with no understanding of the process:

1. Measure the intensity of the feelings associated with an unpleasant memory. Using a scale of 1 to 10. 10 being the highest.

2. Setup phrase – Tapping the Karate Chop (side of hand), state the problem and include an affirmation about you. Example, "Even though I have this fear about speaking in public, I love and completely accept myself." Pairing exposure to the traumatic ordeal with self-acceptance is a well-researched psychological technique.

3. The sequence of tapping points - (1) Top of head (2) Inner eyebrow (3) Side of eye (4) Under eye (5) Under nose (6) Chin (7) Collarbone (8) Under arm.

Repeat stating the emotional event while doing several rounds of the tapping sequence. Check in after two or three rounds to measure the intensity of your feelings. Notice what is different. Continue if there is remaining anxiety. You are aiming for 0, but getting down to 1 or 2 may be sufficient.

This is the short version of the tapping points sequence. There are many variations based on the presenting problem. YouTube has great footage of EFT demonstrations.

## EFT for PTSD

An area where EFT has been working wonders is with our returning war veterans suffering post-traumatic stress disorder

(PTSD). Many vets suffer from hyper vigilance, anger, insomnia, emotional distancing, nightmares and flashbacks. One organization, EFT Universe, filmed a documentary showing how they work with veterans and their families. Their film, "Operation Emotional Freedom the Answer" is graphically candid and demonstrates healing the physical symptoms of emotional trauma by tapping down the high levels of anger and frustration intensity.

---

## Suggested Action You Can Take

If you want to learn more about EFT visit The EFT Universe website. It has a wealth of information, sample cases, educational material and practitioner resources for anyone wishing to learn more about the Emotional Freedom Technique.

# CHAPTER 8

# AROMATHERAPY: A NATURAL WAY TO BOOST YOUR MOOD

**"Those herbs which perfume the air most delightfully"**
**~Francis Bacon**

I love the aroma of turkey roasting on Thanksgiving morning. The smell of pine cones on the fire and apple cider makes me nostalgic on Christmas day. That's because holiday smells have an emotional connection. They bring back wonderful childhood memories. The aromas lift our spirits and make us think of home.

Our sense of smell is the quickest way to change our emotions and boost our mood. And the quickest way to lift your mood and banish fatigue is to energize your home with fragrances you love. The use of essential oils is a natural way to give your home relaxing aromas all year long.

Certain scents distract you from everyday stresses that zap your energy. When you come home weary from the pressures of the day, you need something pleasant and fresh to welcome you. Place a potpourri of citrus oils like lemon, lime, orange and grapefruit in the entranceway. Grapefruit is both soothing and uplifting. Lemons and oranges freshen the air and lighten your mood.

In the kitchen put a couple of drops of essential oils in a pot of water and simmer. Use orange, lime, lemon or grapefruit for a sparkling morning, lavender for a lift in the afternoon, geranium for a soothing midday and rosemary to relief stress. Add rose or jasmine in the dishwashing liquid at night just for pure indulgence.

In the bedroom essential oils like rose, jasmine or ylang-ylang can be mixed with water and sprayed in the air for a romantic atmosphere. To enhance relaxation and sleep use lavender, chamomile or lemongrass. Drop these relaxing oils on a diffuser or light bulb, radiator or humidifier. And you can wash bed linens with these relaxing scents.

In the bathroom put a couple of drops of aromatic oils like lavender, citronella, lemon, cinnamon or bergamot on the cardboard ring inside the toilet paper roll. The cardboard soaks up the essential oil and gently releases the cleansing molecules. These oils keep the room smelling clean and fragrant.

Don't forget the hallway where odors and stale air tend to linger. This is the place we usually greet visitors. We want to make the best first impression. Geranium is an excellent choice when guests are due because it makes them feel good even before they sit down. A few drops of lemon essential oil will make guest say your house has a relaxing atmosphere…even though they won't know why. But you will.

## Suggested Action You Can Take

There are aromatherapy blends to enhance your mood and beyond – from aphrodisiacs to memory boosters. Learn more at http://www.aromatherapy.com/mood_blends.html.

# CHAPTER 9

## A 5 MINUTE MORNING MEDITATION TO LIFT YOUR SPIRITS AND PUT A SMILE ON YOUR FACE

**"Happiness is when what you think, what you say, and what you do are in harmony." ~Mahatma Gandhi**

Have you tried to meditate but gave up because it took too much time? It was boring? You couldn't stop your "mind chatter"? Give mindfulness-based meditation a try. An ancient Eastern practice, mindfulness means being present and passively observing your experience in the very moment you live it.

My favorite way to meditate is by daydreaming:

Set your alarm five minutes earlier tomorrow. When you get up, find a quiet place to sit and gaze out a window. Look up at the sky. Really notice the color and expanse. Follow the shape and movement of the clouds.

Let your thoughts drift as you enjoy the morning stillness. This is your time to focus on what is good in your life – not the worries of yesterday, today or tomorrow.

**Begin** your meditation by focusing on your breathing. The rhythmic rise and fall of your breath. Since breathing has a strong effect on emotional change, it is a natural bridge to begin to meditate. Slow measured breathing has a calming effect.

**Gently** close your eyes and tune into your body. A word will come to you that describes what you are feeling. Calm, relaxed, peaceful, happy, confident. That is your relaxation keyword. Spread the word throughout your body. From the top of your head to the tip of your toes.

**Put** your relaxation key word in a phrase that inspires you to handle stress differently today. For example, *"I am calm and relaxed"* when you are feeling tense and anxious. Use this phrase whenever you need it throughout the day.

*\*Inhale** slowly and mentally repeat, *"I live with a happy heart, a peaceful mind and a playful spirit"*. Stay with it for a minute or two. Inhale deeply and in the privacy of your own mind quietly shout, "I deserve health and happiness!"

Just before you are ready to open your eyes, begin to stimulate that positive energy that is a smile by recalling something you enjoy. Something that makes you feel good. Let the corners of your mouth turn up. **Smile.** Send this smiling energy into every bone and every organ and every nerve and every cell in your body.

**Now take that smiling energy up into your heart.**

Decide what you would like to take with you into your day. Something of a positive, inspiring nature. Open your eyes and start a day you look forward to!

---

## Suggested Actions You Can Take

Ease into meditation slowly. Just by focusing on your breathing you are doing a form of meditation. You are trying to keep your thoughts in the moment – not worrying about yesterday, today or tomorrow.

---

*From Quantum Focusing – Finding the Zone by Michael Ellner and Alan Barsky.

Simplicity is key. All you need is:

➢ A quiet space

➢ A word, sound, thought or observation that inspires you

➢ Five minutes or less

Experience more relaxing meditation when you get your free Bonus Gift: The Calming Breath 5-Minute Guided Meditation Video. Visit http://www.thecalmingbreath.com for access.

# CHAPTER 10

# BONUS: BE A MORE VIBRANT PERSON: HOW TO FIT RELAXATION INTO YOUR BUSY DAY

A daily energizing routine of Breath, Affirmations, Meditation, Visualization and Progressive Relaxation will help you feel your best every day: Bold, Awesome, Motivated, Vibrant and Passionate.

Like many women you multi-task every day juggling the demands of work, home and family. You rarely find time to take a break and de-stress. In fact taking time out to relax is a "guilty pleasure" you can't afford.

But those stress related symptoms...the irritability, fatigue, that run-down depressed feeling ...tell us that "me time" is important for our emotional and physical health. Women who practice relaxation every day are better able to cope with stress related symptoms, illness and disease.

Think you don't have time to fit relaxation in an already too busy day? Five of the most effective stress busters can be done in five minutes or less. Require no special equipment. Just your breath and imagination. All are easy to do and can easily fit into a busy schedule. They are:

**B**reath

**A**ffirmations

**M**editation

**V**isualization

**P**rogressive Relaxation

# Making BAM VP Work For You

## Morning Meditation: Time 5 minutes

Beginning tomorrow morning, don't hit the ground running! Set your alarm five minutes earlier to ease into your day. Meditation is about being in the moment. Not letting worries intrude. This is your time for quiet serenity. Use it to reflect on what is good in your life.

### Affirmations: Time 0 minutes

During your morning cleanse, look into the mirror and say something good about yourself. While it is easy to find superficial faults, this day you will choose to embrace all that is uniquely you. Positive thoughts about yourself to yourself will lift your spirits.

Meanwhile, take a look at the tasks ahead of you this day. State your intention to succeed in all your challenges today. This optimistic view will raise your self-esteem and boost your confidence.

### Breath and Visualization: Time 1 minute

Periodically during the day, ideally every time you change activities, take a minute to relax and recharge. Put the to-do list on hold. Sit comfortably and focus on your breathing. Beginning on the exhalation, take slow deep breaths from the diaphragm. Inhale. Oxygen fills the lungs, circulates throughout the blood stream and triggers the relaxation response. Muscles relax. Breath and heart rate slows.

Close your eyes and visualize a beautiful memory or proud moment. Make it real by noticing the colors, sights, sounds, smells, who you are with, what you are wearing, etc. Visualization encourages the release of "feel good" endorphins. Puts a smile on your lips. Now open your eyes and continue with your day.

### Progressive Relaxation: Time 5 minutes

At the end of a long day this deep muscle massage is a great sleep aid. While lying in bed, tighten and relax each muscle group. Begin with the feet. Then the calves, thighs, stomach and buttocks, arms, fists, shoulders, neck and face. Repeat until you feel tension and fatigue drain from your body.

If physically tightening and relaxing your muscles is uncomfortable, mental relaxation is effective. Concentrate on the area you want to relax. Send your thoughts and imagine yourself enjoying a deep muscle massage with each muscle group.

And there you have it. Five of the most effective stress busters in five minutes or less. Breath, Affirmations, Meditation, Visualization and Progressive Relaxation. All the tools you need to Be A More Vibrant Person (BAM VP). Bold. Awesome. Motivated. Vibrant. Passionate.

# RECAPTURE YOUR JOY OF LIVING

**"You only live once, but if you do it right, once is enough"**
**~Mae West**

I hope you found some useful tips and techniques for relieving the stress in your life. And put them to the test. Don't let your journey end here. Make your well-being a priority today. Schedule some "me time" to relax, refresh, reenergize. Make managing stress a vital part of your daily routine.

Become the BAM VP woman you were meant to be. With a new attitude. Bold, Awesome, Motivated, Vibrant and Passionate!

**Be sure to stop by my website to get your Bonus Gift: The Calming Breath 5- Minute Guided Meditation Video for the most relaxing "me time" experience. Visit http://www.thecalmingbreath.com for access.**

I'd love to hear how Ten Powerful Stress Busters for the BAM VP Woman in You worked for you. And I am always interested in new relaxation methods you'd like to share. Comment on my blog: http://thecalmingbreath.blogspot.com.

Always be good to yourself,

Barbara Mitchell, DCH

# ABOUT THE AUTHOR

**"Nothing happens...but first a dream." ~Carl Sandburg**

Barbara Mitchell, DCH is an Author, Stress Management Consultant, Doctor of Clinical Hypnotherapy and a retired College Administrator. She helps men, women and children experiencing emotional distress, grief, burnout and trauma move through the pain and recapture their joy for living.

Her "BAM VP- Be A More Vibrant Person" techniques were first introduced during an author interview on the Balancing Act on Lifetime Television.

In addition to consulting, Dr. Barbara has created an online relaxation course, Learning the Joy of Relaxation, for the education site Udemy.com.

She enjoys writing, painting, and travel with her husband to sunny beaches, reading the comics (her guilty pleasure) and spending time with her daughter and family members. And most of all she enjoys rediscovering the wonders of the world through the eyes of her two amazing grandchildren.

Be sure to stop by my website to get your Bonus Gift:

**The Calming Breath 5- Minute Guided Meditation Video**

for the most relaxing "me time" experience.

Visit http://www.thecalmingbreath.com for access.